FINDING
AGATES

Dennis Kirouac

ISBN 978-1-0980-1262-5 (paperback)
ISBN 978-1-0980-1264-9 (hardcover)
ISBN 978-1-0980-1263-2 (digital)

Christian Faith Publishing, Inc.
832 Park Avenue
Meadville, PA 16335
www.christianfaithpublishing.com

Printed in the United States of America

INTRODUCTION

In everyone's life there are moments of discovery. This story begins on the shores of Lake Superior tucked away on the northwestern edge of Michigan's Upper Peninsula. There many people from all over the world come to search for an elusive and prized gemstone, the agate. You may be asking, "What is an agate?" Throughout the world, there are many semi-precious stones of which one of them is the agate.

Agate

Ex 28:19, 39:12

Agate is named as the second stone in the third row of the high priest's breastplate. Agates are a form of chalcedony (a fine-grained variety of quartz) that are banded or lined in a variety of patterns of colored layers. Colors range from white to dull yellow, red, brown, orange, blue, black, and gray. The Hebrew word for agate is *shebo* which literally means "to flame, split into tongues." "*Agate*" comes from the Greek word, achates, which is the name of the river in Sicily where agate was mined (www.preciousstonesofthebible.com).

The foundations of the city walls were decorated with every kind of precious stone. The first foundation was jasper, the second sapphire, the third agate, the fourth emerald, the fifth onyx, the sixth ruby, the seventh chrysolite, the eighth beryl, the ninth topaz, the tenth turquoise, the eleventh jacinth, and the twelfth amethyst. The twelve gates were twelve pearls, each gate made of a single pearl. The great street of the city was of gold, as pure as transparent glass. (Revelation 21:19–21, NIV)

Rocks and stones are mentioned throughout the Bible, and many times they are synonymous with truth.

"And I tell you that you are Peter, and on this rock I will build my church, and the gates of Hades will not overcome it" (Matthew 16:18, NIV).

Here we see that Jesus is telling Peter that upon this truth he will build His church.

"So David triumphed over the Philistine with a sling and a stone; without a sword in his hand he struck down the Philistine and killed him" (1 Samuel 17:50, NIV).

Goliath came at David with his own armor. He had his own helmet of salvation, his own breastplate of self-righteousness, and the sword of his own spirit. David launched God's rock of truth which went straight to the source of the problem, right between the eyes where man's thoughts reside, and he used Goliath's own sword to remove this origin of the knowledge of good and evil.

"When they kept on questioning him, he straightened up and said to them, 'Let any one of you who is without sin be the first to throw a stone at her'" (John 8:7, NIV).

Here the people had the rocks of truth about this woman, and according to the Law of Moses, they were within their rights to use these truths on her, but Jesus's answer shows us how we are to handle these truths we find out about each other. We are to lay these truths before Jesus and let Him handle it.

This little book is about the most precious stone of all, the chief cornerstone, Jesus, and all the truths that God has let me find over the years of searching. Some are rough around the edges, some are not, but all are to the glory of God. To me, the definition of glory means the invisible made visible. The invisible nature of God made visible to you and me.

FINDING AGATES

In November of 1958, my parents (Jacques and Hilde Kirouac) made a life changing leap of faith to purchase a small beachside motel/restaurant venue on the shores of Lake Superior. "Johnsons Motel" was located along M-64 halfway from Silver City and the village of Ontonagon, nestled between the Big and Little Cranberry rivers. They moved from the suburbs of Detroit with five children, plus one who would soon join them in February of 1959.

Arriving on a late November day, this seven-year-old was greeted with five to seven-foot waves and snow blowing in my face. As I approached this wild untamed beach with the ice beginning to form, I saw a round patch of sand surrounded by six inches of snow. In the middle of this patch lay a pocket knife with a bluish grey handle. No footprints, no lingering evidence of human contact. I carefully stepped into the circle to collect my welcome to the Lake Superior gift. It was there I felt the Lake accepting me into its family. That memory of the knife stays with me to this day.

* * *

Every action I take has eternal and lasting consequences. I cannot walk the beach without permanently impacting it. The sheer weight and velocity of my steps will compact the sand beneath and cause the grains to create new and permanent scratches on one another. Long after the waves have removed the visible evidence of my steps, the beach has been forever altered by my presence.

> *As iron sharpens iron, so one person sharpens another.* (Proverbs 27:17, NIV)

In life, we all are impacting and being impacted by one another. Be careful how you walk...your steps matter.

Growing up on the shores of Lake Superior, I learned the art of Agate picking. As a child, the constant opportunities of rewards from diligent effort afforded itself every time I walked the beach. Over time, I developed a keen eye to quickly "pick out" an agate no matter how small and with very little effort. This love was also shared by those who lived on the beach, and it grew into a friendly competition amongst neighbors to see who got the largest or most unique agate that week.

Much in the same way, I believe that is what God wants from all of us—to be searchers of the good in everyone we meet. Each of us has value that is unique to them and for us. No one is here on this planet by mistake. Each is here on purpose for a purpose. One must develop a keen eye and heart for this most wondrous hunt. This hunt is also for the things of God which is scattered throughout our path just for the finding.

━━━━━━━━━━━━━━━

"Where your treasure is there you heart will be also" (Matthew 6:21, NIV).

Another word for treasure is valuables. Many things can be valuable—gold, silver, jewels, things, photos, family, your opinions, the possibilities go on and on. Anything of value demands some type of attention, care, and protection. These values "drive our behaviors."

You can look at anyone any time and see what their values are base on by what is seen and heard. The way one dresses, grooms, or voices, all are driven by a set of values which drives those behaviors. When God becomes your treasure, then all the resulting behaviors will follow. Remember it says your heart will follow your treasure. Only in God are you able to handle these true treasures that God wants you to steward. Without God's guidance, these blessings would corrupt and crush us.

During the summer months, many of our motel guests would be found scouring the beach for these precious stones. I remember one particular day when I went down to the beach, which more times than not would lead to the approach of a guest or a mob of guests with handfuls of stones, inquiring "Are any of these agates?" On this particular day, a middle-aged mother was the first in a procession of other family members requesting such assistance.

As I carefully surveyed her bounty, I quickly responded that they were very beautiful stones, but unfortunately there were no agates. Just then I spotted a very large and beautiful agate by her big toe. I immediately told her of it, to which she quickly dropped all the stones and gave her full attention to what was just under her nose. Her excitement quickly disappeared as she strained to locate the prize. She looked up to me with a stunned countenance and blurted out, "Which big toe?"

It was then that I realized that to be able to see the agate, one must first have the agate on the inside. I can only recognize what is already in me first. This is why we must be born again and be filled in the Holy Spirit in order to recognize anything spiritually.

□□□□□□□□

Only by the indwelling presence of God are we able and enabled to give mercy. Mercy "that is, righteous Godly mercy" is not found naturally in the heart of man. This is one of the true attributes and evidences of His Holy Spirit. With His guidance, we will have the ability to see opportunities to give it away. Mercy adds and multiplies as we *divide* with others (please note that in the word *divide,* the words *I* and *die* are hidden in it).

Agate picking in the fall was my most favorite time of the year. Warm pleasant southerly breezes combine with clear, cloudless skies and empty, bug-less beaches. It was like having a secret agate garden and everything is free for the choosing. It felt like heaven had come down to earth, and the day could go on forever.

―――――――

"*What was lost in the Garden was gained back in a garden.*"

What was lost in the garden of Eden was gained back in the garden of Gethsemane.

This is the only place in the Bible where you read about Jesus sweating it. Not only once but three times, Jesus cries out to the Father and inquires if there is another way. But through all this, Jesus says, "Thy will be done," and the rest is history. Nothing—not the denial, scourging, not even the death and resurrection—could have transpired without that tipping point moment of choice. What was lost through a choice in one garden was gained back by a choice in the other.

Remember this, that the only freedom that God has given you is the freedom to chose. Your free will. So you could say that God is pro-choice. But the moment you choose, that choice controls you. In Joshua 24:15 (NIV), we read:

> But if serving the LORD seems undesirable to you, then choose for yourselves this day whom you will serve, whether the gods your ancestors served beyond the Euphrates, or the gods of the Amorites, in whose land you are living. But as for me and my household, we will serve the LORD.

Joshua knew what he was saying. You will always be either "a *servant of* or a *slave to* your choices" once it has been made. Please know that in some choices you can unchoose.

Our restaurant was a quaint building nestled right beside highway M-64. Its knotty pine interior accommodated room for six tables. Bathed in the glow of warm red neon, it was the gathering place of good homecooked meals and even greater conversation. Many a guest would stay late just to visit with my mother Mathilde (Hilde) Kirouac. One such downstate couple was "rock-hounds" who loved our beach and every year would visit faithfully. This relationship began with the receiving of a gift of agates that my mother had given them on their first stay. This gesture led to a package arriving the next Christmas. It was a display of not only her agates but also many other collectable rocks such as African tiger-eye, Wausau moonstone, and smoky quarts, laid out and perfectly sized for the restaurants cozy interior. Future potential "rock-hounds" were educated and encouraged about what an agate looks like.

L ive your life on purpose for a purpose. God has a unique purpose for our lives. There has never been nor will there ever be anyone exactly like you in all of eternity. For such a time as this, you are a "one-up" that God has created for a unique service to which no one else can do. Your lot is to do that "*that*" that God has called you to be and do. God will use various ways to draw and encourage us into His plan. You are God's gift He wishes to share with the world.

Some of the best agate picking days would be those following a lengthy storm. During a storm, the "inventory" would be redistributed, and hopes would be springing up as a new batch would be revealed. Large waves would still be smoothly rolling in as a great cache of rock would be exposed. We would run to the beach to seek what new treasures were to be given up.

"But store up for yourselves treasures in heaven, where moths and vermin do not destroy, and where thieves do not break in and steal" (Matthew 6:20, NIV).

Each person is a warehouse of experiences stored up and regularly inventoried. Boxes marked good times, boxes marked bad times, boxes marked rejection, boxes marked dreams line the walls of their warehouses to which only they have the key.

Outside the warehouse is the storefront which is the area where they display only the treasures that they will allow others to see. From that "front," we can only assume that the treasures displayed represent what is regularly warehoused in the back.

Jesus is asking to go with you behind the counter and into the backroom to do some trading up. He wants to exchange beauty for ashes, courage for fear, faith for doubt, love for self-hatred and shame.

"What in your warehouse?"

God will use storms in life to turn over new agates of truth to put in your warehouse of experience. Every storm, no matter how long, is an opportunity to gain new treasures.

Over the years I learned of various techniques of agate picking. These methods may vary seasonally, but all are effective in their own right. Some of these are stooping over browsing for those with good backs. A popular way is the stay and sift in one spot. My personal favorite was "crabbing." In late July, the lake temperature as well as its temperament would be warm and calm. I would be found with a face mask on my float, "crabbing for agates." My family would see me headed to the beach early, and the word would go out that I would be gone until further notice and not to be disturbed. I would often fall asleep and be found floating as far as a mile away. I would be seen returning with a prize bounty in hand and sporting major sunburn to one half of my body. This two-tone look was my badge of achievement.

J ust like agates, truths are precious, and we should all develop techniques to find them. Learning to bow down and be humble gets us into the position to see these truths. Sometimes we need sit and sift in one spot or just crab about for it. But in all cases we need to be searching. In *Matthew 7:7 (NIV)*, we read, *"Ask and it will be given to you; seek and you will find; knock and the door will be opened to you."*

Remember hearts, minds, and parachutes all work better when their open. God rewards of those who diligently seek Him. And what is the reward? It's Him!

I must confess that agates were not the only item on the collection menu. Pretty stones were as well. I would pick many for my children's church class and place them in a large glass bowl. Then I would share how each stone is unique and different, just like people. I would then add water, and the stones would suddenly appear even more beautiful and special, just like when God's love is added, we too become more beautiful and special. At the end of the lesson, each child would get to pick out a stone they liked to take home.

"You like someone because, but you love some although." God loves us although. His love washes over us all the time—just like the waves that washed over these stones.

It took many years of searching for a large white agate. Not a chip but large. Every time I would go out, my hope was to finally get "the great white whale." I even expanded my range from between the Big and Little Cranberry rivers to include the Green Park and Union Bay. Finally the moment came when I beheld it. Through the mask while crabbing, I yelled in excitement, forgetting I was underwater! (Almost drowned.) What joy I felt. Patient effort and persistent paid off.

What has struck me is that in great abundance, one must still hunger and thirst. With all the abundance of beautiful stones, I was still striving to find a one of a kind unique stone which would be of a special value over all the rest. This vision was the value that drove my efforts. I spent hours searching and researching areas in a confident hope that soon I would find.

I believe that the Bible verse that God rejoices over one who repents is much like that. God is always searching for you and I. He never gives up no matter what. Why? Because we are a valuable one of a kind that he cherishes. In the whole of the universe, all of humankind is but a few agates scattered on the beach of this earth, and I believe God is continually looking to and fro for those who are shining.

Of course I was not the only one in my family who was drawn to the lake—my mother as well. She not only collected stones but also driftwood which was in plentiful supply. She had a unique talent to create driftwood and stone centerpieces which she would display in the restaurant. Many a driftwood piece destined for the bonfire was rescued and repurposed.

One day, one of the guests asked if one particular piece was for sale. She had never thought that her art would be anything but therapy of love. Soon a microbusiness was born. It is amazing how bits and pieces of broken and random debris could be salvaged into something unique, beautiful, and create value.

A line from an old Christian song reads, *"Something beautiful something good/ all my confusion He understood./ All I had to offer Him was brokenness and strife/ and He made something beautiful out of my life."* God is in the business of transforming us, salvaging us and creating a one-of-a-kind centerpiece to hold His love.

The lake offers more than just stones, it has various moods, its home for inspiration for all who search. I recall one summer evening when a gifted violinist walked onto the beach as if a stage and began to play a beautiful melody at the lake's edge. Facing the setting sun, it seemed as if he was playing a lullaby as the sun sank slowly into the sleep of the night. Guests were drawn to this most holy moment, tears flowed, and hearts were lifted as the sun finally slipped away into a glorious afterglow. As the music continued to fill the air, guests began to spontaneously sing and applaud. What a wonderful experience to share in a moment of pure love between God and man.

From the rising of the sun to the place where it sets, the name of the LORD is to be praised. (Psalm 113:3, NIV)

I wake up every morning to the dawning of a new day. Throughout the day, I see and respond to what is reflected by this light. My job is to live each day as if it were my last day, and at the setting of the sun to, "having left nothing on the table," I want my light and song of every word and deed to leave a lasting afterglow on whoever and whatever in Jesus's mighty name.

Living on the shores of Lake Superior was an awesome child-hood experience. Being at a resort site afforded one exposure to visitors from all over the world. It was a place where many became repeat guests because as they would say it, *"The lake is calling and I must come."* Much of my world was shaped from conversations overheard during evening restaurant chats that guests would have with my mother. From my vantage point back in the kitchen as the chief dish and bottle washer, all manner of opinions would fly—politics, religion, family issues were discussed. It seemed that this setting had an effect on many where they felt safe to be themselves. They often would say that they had forgotten who they really were, and somehow they've reconnected with their true self.

The lake air also had an effect. Many guests would inquire what time the restaurant would be opening and that they were early birds who were always *"up and at 'em."* The next morning, they would stumble in around 10:30a.m., inquiring if they can have the room for another day because they had never slept so well. Lake air, good food, and conversation often led to peace of mind and soul.

Every word is a seed no matter how small and is powerful and causes change. The parable of the mustard seed come to mind, as well as what Zig Ziegler said about how a field is just like our mind. The field doesn't care what you plant. It only multiplies whatever has been planted. Our minds are the same, it doesn't care what is planted. It will only multiply what is sown. We are both the field and farmer. Everywhere we go is an opportunity to sow; however, we need to take every thought sown captive unto the obedience of Christ. If we don't, it will capture us and take where we don't want to go and pay a price we never thought we have to pay for longer than we ever thought we have to pay it. I was very fortunate to be overhearing healthy and caring dialogue from heart to heart.

Sometimes finding an agate was a spectacular find. Late one August evening was such a moment. A major storm from the northwest had just blown through and the lake was all riled up and the clouds were fragmented in low-hanging black chunks scattered across the whole of the sky. The sun was setting and shafts of light shot out from between each cloud and as you looked down the beach, you could see segments of beach that were alit brightly as if on fire. One of these shafts lay just a short distance in front of me. This contrast of dark and light is one of the most rare and wonderful sides of the lakes personality.

From where I stood, a lone, red glow like a beacon of a lighthouse caught my eye. I began to run as fast I could, hoping to get to it before the ever-changing light, and the waves would remove it and hide it forever. It turned out to be one of biggest and most beautiful agates I ever found. It was truly a miracle. Imagine it, light that has been trapped for eons finally escapes from the sun's grip, and eight minutes later, it splashes up on a shore to illuminate a lone rock for a searcher to see. I felt as if all of heaven and earth had orchestrated this moment.

"Yet I am writing you a new command; its truth is seen in him and in you, because the darkness is passing and the true light is already shining" (1 John 2:8, NIV).

Jesus is the light of the world, and just like the sun, His light is new and fresh—never recycled—always pure from Him, and whatever He reveals, we should run to quickly find what He is shedding His light (truth) on.

I wonder how many rocks I picked over the years, thinking it an agate, but by holding it to the light, closer scrutiny would reveal its true identity which resulted in sending it back to where it came from. No matter how good at initial identifying I got, I still fell for the same false appearances.

> *"Hope deferred makes the heart sick, but a longing fulfilled is a tree of life"* (Proverbs 13:12, NIV).

There can be a fine line between truth and lie. A lie can look so right on the surface, and yet upon closer examination, its truth is revealed. One thing I've learned is that man is made to run on truth not lies. We do not handle lies very well. In fact we will handle an ugly truth much better than a beautiful lie.

There have been times when I would be going to and fro doing various chores and tasks. Lost in my own world of busyness so much so that I didn't even notice the "Great Lake" in front of me. Every once in a while, I would catch myself and stop and say, "Oh my gosh, this is Lake Superior! This is a one of the great lakes, and I get to live on it!"

T here is a term, "Indifference through saturation," which applies to all of life. Just as it states, we can become numb to what is in front of us just by over exposure. We need to continually renew our appreciation of its significance or we will become indifferent. This especially applies to relationships both with God and others. We need to stop and look with fresh eyes. This also is an important tip in agate picking.

In late July, we would get days of winds which create large waves and warm surf. We would go out to the first sandbar where the waves would curl and body surf back great distances. On these days, we could see where the second and third sandbars were because of the lighter water coloration. On calm days, we would swim out to find them. This was always a very long swim to the second sandbar where the water would be up to your chin or eyes. The third would most likely be a foot over your head, and you would have to bounce off the bottom to show where it was. Between the bars, the water would be very deep but clear so you could see where large boulders would be scattered on the bottom. I was always hoping for a boulder-sized agate.

God's Word is clear no matter how deep we dive in. Sometimes we have to get away from the shallow shores of familiarity and get a fresh new perspective. Peter getting out of the boat is one of these examples. He was asked to leave his familiar fellowship (that's fellows in the same ship) and step into a situation where he would be in uncharted waters and in over his head. Only by keeping his eyes on Jesus could he keep his head above the situation. Never be afraid to swim out into deeper waters of faith to explore new sandbars of understanding. Just remember to keep your eyes on Jesus.

Winter on Lake Superior would put a definite stop on agate picking but not on agate tumbling. My parents had purchased a pair of "rock tumblers" which was located, due to noise levels in our utility room, where our motel service supplies were stored. We learned how the different grit level of slurry would affect the surface of the stone, and as these grits, over long periods of tumbling time, would produce an even depth scratches to surface of the stones. We would change these grits out to finer and finer until a smooth reflective surface revealing the fine lines of the agate would be attained. This is of course a microlevel of what the lake itself does all the time.

W inter in our lives is much the same. We are constantly being tumbled in slurry of gritty people and situations. Scratched and wounded, we over time have our rough edges worn down until we reflect our true inner self. All of life is a tumbler experience where every moment is a refining moment where over time we get the chance to reflect the light of Christ to a dark world.

Going out on what we called icebergs (really shelf ice) was an adventure and an unrealized danger. Large volcano-like formations would be spread out in rows along the first and later the second sandbars. On windy days, you could see the waves shooting up and out of these spouts, flinging water and round balls of ice down its sides. Like freezing lava, this would build up to very large mountains with ice caves and cliffs, which later when everything was completely frozen and no water was left, we would go out and explore. I remember going for naps in some of these caves. One year, the lake froze over, and there were pressure breaks about a half mile out. I walked out took pictures of slabs of clear, blue ice standing straight up. What a sight to behold.

The tempest comes out from its chamber, the cold from the driving winds.

The breath of God produces ice, and the broad waters become frozen.

He loads the clouds with moisture; he scatters his lightning through them.

At his direction they swirl around over the face of the whole earth to do whatever he commands them.

He brings the clouds to punish people, or to water his earth and show his love. (Job 37:9–13, NIV)

It was times like this that I would be humbled at just how this lake demonstrated the magnificence and power of God.

Deep winter in the Upper Peninsula is a most amazing experience. One night the temperature had fallen to almost minus forty below, as I walked out onto the ice-covered beach, the sound of the hard scrunch of the snow beneath my boots seemed to announce my arrival to all of nature. The moon was full and an utter silence stretched out on the lake ice, so quiet and still, it was as if everything had stopped. The mountain and the lake appeared as a stage which was brightly lit by the moon and stars as the northern lights danced above like an ever-shimmering curtain about to be pulled to reveal a heavenly host.

God is like the sun and Jesus is like the moon who reflects the full glory of his father's light into this dark world. Be still and know he is God.

Each season would bring new stories about the lake and its surroundings. Spring would be exciting with the ice flows going out from the rivers, especially the Ontonagon. There was always a pool betting on which date the river would "go out." April 1 (April Fool's Day), 1963, after a record-cold winter combined with unseasonably warm weather caused the river to launch out and pile up at its mouth causing the worst flooding in the history of the village, I recall standing on M-64 near the Horner Waldorf paper mill where the water's edge lay. In the distance, I could see a great sea surrounding the entire downtown. Later that Memorial Day, the landmark Elk Hotel burned to the ground. By the time Fourth of July came, nobody wanted to be around for fear of what would be coming next.

L ife around Lake Superior revealed power of nature in a way that one could easily see how small we all are and how the thought of being in control of anything was a mere allusion. I recall standing on the Ontonagon swing bridge as the ice began to go out one spring. The bridge shook as ice slabs as large as cars slammed into it. All was ice. As far as one could see, upriver, no waters, just a moving, grinding freight train of ice. God's will is much like that—breaking loose and flowing forward with unstoppable force.

Spring smelt season brought out neighbors from their winter hibernations. They would show up to stand alongside the various rivers and creeks, dipping for these six to eight-inch beauties. Beach fires we alight as friendships were renewed, and the latest news was shared in a sort of a family reunion. There was always room for one more dip net as there was plenty of smelt to go around. Many a neighbor was found putting smelt into another's bucket that was having a poor go of it.

*T*here is an old question, "Is the glass half empty or is it half full?" At a very young age, we learned the answer to that one is "That depends, are you drinking or are you pouring?" One should serve from their saucer and not their cup. It was out of the overflow we share. God is all about giving, adding, through overflow.

There are seven seasons of the year in the Upper Peninsula. The usual winter, spring, summer, fall. There was also smelt, black fly, and hunting.

Black fly is by far the worst. We would have to brave these flying demons as they circled about tirelessly. Our great joy was to go up to the entry point of the camp ground at Union Bay where they had the large fly paper trap set just to watch and see these pests get theirs.

E ven in the land of milk and honey, one must still milk the cows and fight off the bees.

There are other beautiful agate stories I grew up with on this Great Lake. My family also shared in this awesome adventure. Linda, Vivian, Gary, Sharon and Christine, who was the only true Yooper by birth—all experienced this in their own unique and special way. Each were shaped and molded into the finest people I know, and all are an inspiration to me of true followers of Jesus. It amazes me how we can be so physically apart, and yet when we gather together as family, we can pick up right where we left off. This includes their spouses as well. Oh, the stories one could tell, but the names would have to be changed to protect the innocent.

*O*ur restaurant was the site of many a family gathering where all would sit and join in family worship and sharing. These were some of our parents' most precious moments, to see all the children with their children praising as one.

The Big Cranberry River was a regular destination throughout the year. Swimming, fishing, hunting, trapping, bonfires, canoeing, rafting, skating, and exploring were experiences where many hours were spent learning. One such memory was when the river was high and running out into the lake one day and totally closed off the next day. I and the other boys of the neighborhood would count off three days before we would attempt to fish. Our hope would be that a school of northern pike would have slipped in to the river that night and would now be trapped and very hungry. Our plan was to meet up in the morning and have a shotgun start where each would sprint to our favorite spots in hopes of winning bragging rights for the largest as well as the most fish, followed by a group fish fry at one of the boy's home that afternoon.

One time, I had high hopes because I had just purchased a brand-new Dardevle spoon. I remember running to the big bend area of the river, and while still running, I let fly with the first cast which led to an instant strike of a thirty-inch pike. The strike was so hard that the red-and-white paint came off, turning it into a silver spoon. Of course, later in life, I learn that the spoon was most likely to have been defective, but that day all of us were in awe.

One of the fruits of the Holy Spirit is the patience. Just like Jesus was in the tomb for three days, we need to wait upon the Lord to renew our strength. Webster's describes *patience* as the capacity to accept or tolerate delay, trouble, or suffering without getting angry or upset. Another fruit is self-control. This river taught us many life lessons.

The lake had many moods which influenced all who lived near and far. One such mood was a wild anger, which you learned respect, fear, and awe. I recall seeing huge logs being tossed about like matchsticks and many a fishing boat being rocked and rolled from side to side as they tried to make their way for safe harbor. When the Edmund Fitzgerald sank, our hearts did as well. Only miles from safer waters of White Fish Bay, it lost its battle.

Life has all types of weather to throw at you and especially the storms that blow in and rock you over and over. Like a lighthouse, God is always pointing the way to safe harbor of His presence.

In later years when my wife Kathie and I would visit the old motel as guests, we would love to sit and sip tea and read, all the while gale force winds would be buffeting outside. The roar of wind and waves would make you want to sit by the fire and tuck in quietly while sitting it out. This quest for coziness would evoke childhood memories of feeling safe and sheltered from the elements.

*E*ven though everything about you may be in chaos, God always offers a peace in the midst of the storm. Just sit tight and wait upon Him. Be still and know that He is God.

As I watch wave after waves pound the shore, it reminds me of Alberta Mannan. Alberta grew up just a few houses down the beach from us. I first met her one morning as she and her father walked the beach. Alberta's father was a very kind man who was very proud of his Down's syndrome toddler who's ever-present smile would warm your heart. Both Alberta's parents would pass away early in her life, and my mother as well as my sister Linda would eventually become legal guardians for her. She is fully considered one of our family.

One thing that Alberta has taught me was that whenever you asked her, "How are things going?" She would reply with a smile, "Excellent." One of our fondest memories is of her sitting on the water's edge in her flowered bathing cap, armed with a stick swatting at the big waves as they rolled in over her and yelling, "Back, back!" as if taming the waves. This battle royal was a continuous fight she championed throughout the summer swimming season.

*E*ach *generation* is like a wave which takes its turn rising up in a crescendo to launch forward onto the beach of life to make its mark, only to slowly retreat to allow the next generation to have a go of it. The rocks of truth each generation reveals can be lost to the next generation.

There is Scripture verse about the new and old wine skins. What jumps out is the fact the wineskin represents a "capacity" for something, and the wine represents the spirit of belief. The ability to stretch and therefore increase ones capacity is very important in order to remain viable as one's belief increases. In the natural, the old wine-skin which is already stretched to its max will be unable to stretch any further and eventually will burst and the wine of belief will spill out leaving the skin ruined an unusable.

That is why we must be born again.

When a child is born, he or she represents a new capacity which is very pliable and stretchable. As they grow up, they become set (no further stretch available) in their ways of thinking and doing.

Being born again represents that newness of faith. The Holy Spirit begins to stretch us in new ways, and we find out that we have new capacities for love, forgiveness, service, trust, belief, and hope. It is written that to each man has been given a measure of faith. What is your measure (capacity)? How about "I can do all things through Christ who strengthens me"? Jesus often said, "O yea of little faith," so what is your capacity? Remember one should realize that they are being born anew in every moment, so this means that as our faith increases, so does our capacity to contain.

Unfortunately this capacity for each generation's applies for evil as well and what for one generation is a limit, for the next is just fine and they will make room for it.

There are two seasons that sum up the total of the other seasons in the Upper Peninsula—shoveling and swatting. The latter season refers to its state bird AKA the mosquito, and shoveling which refers to the fact that we have nine-month winter and three months of tough sledding.

Our first winter was an eye-opening experience. We had twelve-foot-high area light that was hung from a single wood pole sporting a six-foot arm with forty-five-degree bracing. The snow drift which came directly from the lake buried the whole light. For many years, we had a major blizzard every January 28 (my birthday), forcing the rare closing of school which made all my siblings very happy.

On this day one year, our next-door neighbors Elmer and Mabel Mongeau, who had lost their only son on the beaches of Normandy, had tragedy strike again with Elmer passing from a heart attack from shoveling by hand when his snow thrower failed to start. I had a special relationship with the two of them which started when I dispatched a pesky woodchuck who resided under their garage with a single shot from my .22 caliber rifle. This "sure-shot" landed me the nickname of Matt from Mabel's favorite western TV show called *Gunsmoke*. This in turn earned her the name of Miss Kitty who also starred in the show. From that time on, I took it upon myself that all shoveling, mowing, and other help she needed would be done by me.

"Religion that God our Father accepts as pure and faultless is this: to look after orphans and widows in their distress and to keep oneself from being polluted by the world" (James 1:27, NIV).

J ust like looking for agates, we need to be looking for precious opportunities to pick up and cherish. These opportunities may be found on the other side of the world or right next door.

From our beach, you can see the Porcupine Mountains slipping down to the big lake. High behind the main bluff is Lake of the Cloud, a premier tourist destination. One amazing thing about this place is how the sheer beauty and majesty would evoke a sense of awe. There could be fifty or more people up there, and they would be talking in whispers as if a loud noise might cause this sense of peace and serenity to take wing. The walk up to its summit felt like you were being ushered up to God's throne.

* * *

Your love, LORD, reaches to the heavens, your faith-
    fulness to the skies.
Your righteousness is like the highest mountains,
    your justice like the great deep.
You, LORD, preserve both people and animals.
How priceless is your unfailing love, O God!
People take refuge in the shadow of your wings.

God's presence is a place where that kind of awe can be experienced.

Hidden in the middle of the Porcupine Mountains is an aptly named lake called Mirror Lake. It's a fair hike down from Lake of the Clouds or up from the South Boundary road which weaves its way through the center of the state park. Many hikers make it a highlight destination where two primitive log cabins are available for night stays in the Heart of the Porkies. Quiet and serene, this is a very popular site for silence and reflection

> *Do not merely listen to the word, and so deceive yourselves. Do what it says. Anyone who listens to the word but does not do what it says is like someone who looks at his face in a mirror and, after looking at himself, goes away and immediately forgets what he looks like. But whoever looks intently into the perfect law that gives freedom, and continues in it—not forgetting what they have heard, but doing it—they will be blessed in what they do.* (James 1:22–25, NIV)

When I get up in the morning and place myself in front of the mirror, I go there with the expressed intention to respond to whatever is reflected back to me. The mirror only reflects my condition; it does not judge my condition. The Bible is the mirror to my soul, and when I open it up, I open it with the expressed intention to respond to whatever is reflected. The Bible does not judge, it only reflects my condition. We too are mirrors to each other, not to judge only to reflect.

Tucked away at the most western edge of the Porcupines is a gem called the Presque Isle River. This river carves its way through old growth pines and hemlocks of both the Ottawa National and Porcupine Mountain State forests. There are nine waterfalls scattered along its forty-two-plus mile course and make you feel like you are in the garden of Eden. No matter what season of the year, it's like seeing it for the first time every time.

Many hours were spent fishing, picnicking, and of course rock picking where it empties into Lake Superior.

There is an old Christian song that goes

> *"I've got a river of life flowing out of me!*
> *Makes the lame to walk, and the blind to see.*
> *Opens prison doors, sets the captives free!*
> *I've got a river of life flowing out of me!"*

God's love is new every moment just like the Presque Isle, it flows from heaven to earth carving a path from His heart to yours.

On the northwestern edge of our motel stands a giant jack pine. Like an elder statesman, it is a landmark showing the boundary between beach and lake. On calm days, I would climb up to see the major boulders that lay beneath the lakes glassy surface. Everything seemed small from this perspective. On windy days, the needles would make a soft breath-like sound that soothed the harshness of the the roaring waves, like a mother calming hcr crying child. This lone pine stands as witness of over two hundred years of history. I always felt like I was visitor when in its presence. I often would imagine what it must be like to be standing and being a silent observer of all who called this place home.

*G*od's *Word stands* the test of time. All types of ideas and opinions roar at it only to be calmed and comforted with a still small voice. Climb up into his branches to see things from His perspective.

Eat from the tree of life and be forever fed.

What happens on the beach doesn't necessarily stay at the beach. Often I would discover tracks from the animals which would frequent the shoreline in search of food and water. This was especially true for the Potato and Floodwood Rivers which laid east of where we lived. Whenever my search found me in those areas, I would keep a wary eye for sign. Up from these two rivers were two farms which hosted apple orchards which were the favorite foraging sites in the fall. There the battle between the trees and the bears would be waged. As a young man, I always felt kind of sorry for the trees that could not defend themselves.

───────────────

*T*hose orchards, however, taught me a tremendous life lesson. All of life is about fruit. The *talos* (purpose) of the tree is to bear fruit. Fruit represents the end of a process or a final maturing. Fruit does not look like anything like the tree itself but is made to be pleasing and offer benefit to another. Its sole purpose is for consumption through its destruction. However, within this fruit lies the seed of the continuance of the root. The tree must withstand and endure all kinds of constant trials, weather, and pestilence, even bears which tear up these trees to get at its fruit, only to walk off and scat out the seeds which then starts the journey all over again in a new location. At the end, we must all realize we are here on the planet to bear fruit—not only our progeny but the fruits of the Spirit, which contains the seeds of love, joy, peace, patience, kindness, goodness, faithfulness, gentleness, and self-control. I believe that when God told Adam and Eve to be fruitful and multiply, He meant these fruits as well.

One constant companion of the beach is the ever-rolling waves. The waves can be gentle and playful at times and ferocious and dangerous the next. Without waves, agates would never be exposed nor could they be polished.

One of my fondest memories of growing up was hearing the gentle waves barely visible to the eye making a slight swooshing sound. This was especially relaxing at night. I could hear this lakes lullaby from my bedroom window which was less than a hundred feet from the shore. The lake made its presence known all the time weather in large or small ways; it was always letting me know it was there. To me, it was like the waves were the lake's way of breathing in and out.

━━━━━━━━━━━━

One thing that we all have in common is that we all live from breath to breath. It doesn't matter what you breathed twenty years ago, let alone twenty seconds ago, it's the breath you are taking now that really counts.

Prayer is as natural as breathing. It is the great exchange from our heart to God's heart. We exhale our weakened, stale air only to inhale back a new and living breath from God. Like the ever constant natural rhythm of waves, this vital back-and-forth is what all life needs to function and flourish from moment to moment, both in the natural and in the spiritual.

There is something about a fire on the beach—the mix of shadows, and flickering lights dancing all about to the tune of the sounds of the crackle of the fire harmonizing with the soft whisper of the lake. The smell of the smoke mixed with the scents of poplar and pine carried on the breezes provided an elixir which seemed to calm the most troubled of hearts.

Perfect strangers would gather around and slowly be drawn into a sort of dimly lit safe space where you strain to make out facial expressions, yet through the clarity of their voices, you could see into the beauty of their souls.

Guests would often begin to share about the most important things in their lives such as family, hopes, and dreams.

It's amazing how everyone sitting around and staring at the same fire would be drawn into an experience of true, tender vulnerability and openness.

The Bible says God is light, and in Him there is no darkness. Imagine you and I are standing before the Lord. Being that He is the light of the world and of course, we are not, if I take my gaze off Him and placed it on you, I would see that you cast a shadow. All have sinned and fall short of the glory of God (Rom 3:23).

When we look at each other, we will see that we all cast shadows, but I believe that we are supposed to look at each other through the reflection in Jesus's eyes. It also says that the eyes are the window to the heart. Let us look at each other through Jesus's eyes which is the window to His heart.

Believe it or not, experts say that Lake Superior has diamonds. To date, there are no commercial efforts to mine diamonds, but geologists say there is historical data to support it. Whether you would be able to find them on the beach, I don't know, but I was always hoping for such a prize. Some things that I learned about these beauties are that there are four *C*s of diamonds—cut, color, clarity, and carat-weight.

Most important of these characteristics is the *cut* to gather and reflect the most light possible. Light performance is measured by three factors—brilliance, fire, and sparkle.

Without a high-cut grade, even a diamond of high quality can appear dull and lifeless. A diamond cut poorly and too deep can face-up smaller than it actually is.

After diamond cut, diamond *color* is the second most important characteristic to consider.

Thirdly is *clarity*, which is the assessment of small imperfections on the surface and internally. The surface flaws are called blemishes, and internal defects are known as inclusions. These tiny, natural blemishes and inclusions are microscopic and do not affect a diamond's beauty in any way. Diamonds with the least and smallest inclusions receive the highest clarity grades.

Diamond *carat* is often misunderstood and refers to a diamond's weight, not necessarily its size.

The four *C*s are the same for all relationships whether a person or a church. Jesus is the author and finisher of faith. We each represent a one up facet of Jesus which we have been custom cut in a one-up way to reflect His glory (glory means the invisible made visible). This cut will produce a brilliance, fire, and sparkle to light a dark world. We each display a color of His love. Even though we have tiny, natural blemishes and inclusions, His grace covers it and does not affect His beauty in any way.

My mother was a night owl. She would be up doing either work or making new creations with her lake treasures. With six of us underfoot, coupled with a business to manage, this was probably the only "sane time" she could find for herself. She would leave the motel sign light on all night. The welcoming of the warm, red glow would be a virtual beacon to travelers.

I remember one winter night; my mother and I were up playing cards while a gale force blizzard raged outside. We heard a pounding on our door. There stood a half-frozen snow-covered snowmobiler. He had gone out earlier and had flipped his machine. He thought that he was going to perish. He had wandered for hours and traveled quite some distance before he made out a faint glimmer of the neon. In the Upper Peninsula, everyone looks out for one another. Over the years, many a weary traveler fixed their gaze on that silent sentinel in the distance where they would find a warm and welcoming safe haven.

Life is a lot like wandering in a snowstorm in the dead of night. We have no idea what lies ahead or even if we are headed in the right direction. We don't know whether we should go into the wind or with it. All we do know is there is a strong desire to give up and just let it bury us. When all seems lost, we see a light in the distance, and a spark of hope ignites in our heart. There is a focus for us to fix our eyes upon.

Jesus is the light of the world. A line from and old hymn reads, "Turn your eyes upon Jesus,/ look full in His wonderful face,/ and the things of this world will grow strangely dim/ in the light of His glory and grace." Remember the first thing God created was light. Let him who has eyes, let him see.

Every once in a while, a guest would come into our lives and make such an impact that they would become extended family. Just such guests came in the form of Dale and Marion. Hailing from Grand Rapids Michigan, the likelihood of these senior citizens ever meeting my parents was very unlikely because they drove a pickup camper. Dale had come down with chicken pox while visiting "God's country." They somehow wound up at our motel so that Marion could better care for him while he convalesced. Marion was a clone of my mother; both short, take-charge women who weren't afraid to speak up. Between the two of them, Dale's recovery went very well. When they went to settle up with my parents, they found that there would be no charges. This so touched them that they would often return to visit. They would camp at the motel.

One time, I guided them to Victoria Dam powerhouse to do some white-water fishing. It didn't take long until Marion had gotten a snag in the rocks, and she lost her artificial bait. I helped her re-bait only to have her snag two more times. The fourth attempt happened almost immediately upon casting.

Frustrated and disgusted, Marion announced that she was heading back to the camper, and that was that! She reeled about set the rod on her shoulder as a soldier would a rifle and marched back toward the camper. She was just going to let her line snap and was not interested in the least to try and save her bait.

I looked out and followed the ever-stretching line, waiting to hear the snap when all of a sudden I saw a huge tail flash out of the water. This fish was at least three feet long. I yelled out to Marion, who upon seeing this river monster began to run away in fear.

I threw down my rod and ran to the river's edge, hoping to flick this behemoth onto the bank. Just as I began to straddle the fish, the hook shot out of its mouth and went straight onto my right arm.

So there I was, one foot trying to kick the fish unto to shore while being hooked to a yelling, frantic senior bolting for the camper. Over in seconds, the fish got away, and I got a story and a scar. Marion said later that she at least caught a sucker.

*I*n life, there will be times when all your efforts will fail, and somehow you will be on the hook for it. Just remember when it comes to God, "If it God's will, it's God's bill." You will never be left hanging because He hung for you.

Greenwood Falls was one of my most favorite swimming holes. Located several miles upstream from Silver City on the Big Iron River, it was a step back in time. Water from the Porcupine Mountains would snake back and forth across expansive layers on basalt rock as it attempted to find its way to its destination of Lake Superior. Some spots were two hundred to three hundred feet across. Pools of still water were scattered about where the high spring run-offs had retreated for the summer season. Sign of wildlife abounded everywhere, especially bear.

During haying season, I and other boys would meet up at Greenwoods after a long, hard, hot day to sit under the falls. The water would be warmed by the dark rock, and we could be found sitting and almost sleeping under the watchful eye of a full moon. What a special Upper Peninsula retreat spa owned and operated by God.

Just like the Big Iron, "the paths of least resistance make both men and rivers crooked." Many are the path of shortcuts and surrogates which all lead away from God's presence. The Bible is full of accounts where a vision of God's plan is revealed, and the recipient tries to bring this vision to fulfillment by and through their efforts. Abraham and Sarah is a great example. God said they were going to have a child late in their lives. They believed. This process took another twenty-five years to fulfill, meanwhile they grew impatient and made an Ishmael out of the whole thing. Shortcuts and surrogates never work, they only compound and hamper.

I am ever grateful for the decisions my parents made to purchase the motel/restaurant on Lake Superior. Growing up at a business allowed we children to develop good work ethics, as well to be great hosts. We developed the ability to be accommodating and easily imposed upon with a pleasant attitude. It was fun to provide help and assistance from extra towels to directions to Lake of the Clouds or the local dump which was the best spot to see the bears. The real reward was when they returned regaling about their experiences.

Not all our efforts were so easily successful. Some guests had to be won over or better yet run over by the realities. I remember one guest being very vocal about the fact that we didn't have air conditioning. My mother tried very gently to explain why we didn't when all of a sudden the wind shifted from the south to north, and the temperature dropped twenty degrees. The guest grew very silent and then said to my mother, "I see your point."

Jesus said that to be the greatest in His kingdom, one must be a servant of all. God has sent us His Holy Spirit to be our guide in all things. He is a gentleman and will not dominate or manipulate to get His way.

God resists the proud but gives grace to the humble. Being a servant allows us the opportunity to come along side others and bless them with the gift of assistance.

A life lesson I learned by being raised in the Upper Peninsula tourist industry is how everyone would look out for one another; "why compete for dimes when you can cooperate for dollars." During the short three month summer period our motel—restaurant was extremely busy. One year we experienced twenty-six continuous days of no vacancies. We were usually amongst the first to fill up because of the restaurant convenience. However, before my mother would turn on the "No Vacancy" light, she would always call the other motels down the road to find out what accommodations they still had available and as guests arrived she would network with them and secure places for these late comers.

"And if I go and prepare a place for you, I will come back and take you to be with me that you also may be where I am." (John 14:3, NIV)

Jesus has gone out before all of mankind and has prepared a place. All we have to do is just come. He will never have a "no vacancy" sign on.

Nestled high in the Porcupine Mountains lays Lake of the Clouds. Resting between a gap produced by two ridges, it is fed from the east and exits to the west via the carp river to empty into Lake Superior.

All of life is about the gap. The gap is that space produced when your perceived current situation, and your perceived preferred expectations are not on the same page.

Imagine a line, and in the middle of it, you place a dot representing your current situation. Next on the same line, place two more dots equally distant from the center dot. The dot to your left represents *"your less than < experience"* of your current perceived expectations; the right-hand dot represents *"your more than > experience"* of your current perceived expectations. In either case, this gap demands some type of fill in order to satisfy this gap. In one case, say in the *less than* < situation, we fill it with responses like anger, rage, disappointment, or depression. In the other case, we fill it with over flowing exuberance or joy.

⬚⬚⬚⬚⬚⬚⬚⬚⬚

According to the law given by Moses, it is expected that an eye for an eye and a tooth for a tooth. So we would expect that a less than experience should demand as less than response, yet Jesus says that we are to love our enemies and to turn the other cheek in a *more than > response* to the *less than* < experience.

Just like the notes to music, the gaps demand either major or minor fills or a heart which fills between ridge the beats. We need to take every thought captive unto the obedience of Christ, and we are to choose to fill it with unconditional grace. Remember Jesus fills us to overflowing in order for you and I to fill others.

Hunting season was of course my favorite time of the year. Hunters from all over would descend upon our motel, and from November 15 through the 30, all kinds of personalities from all walks of life would come together around this one common denominator. It was a wonderful and humorous experience to sit in the corner of the restaurant to hear hunting stories of renown. The first liar didn't have a chance.

One story happened to a hunter who was on his very first hunt. He had gotten the very best gear available to insure him of success especially a lever action 30–30 Winchester. On opening day, his hunting partners had kick out a big buck which headed toward this hunter's location, waiting to hear shots ring out from his new rifle. They heard only silence.

They quickly ran to find out what had happened and to see if he was okay. When they arrived, they saw a shaking, quivering, bright-eyed man. One of his friends shouted out, "Did you see him?"

He answered in a still quaky voice, "I missed! I emptied my gun on him and I missed!"

The others looked down, and there in the snow lied all his unfired bullets. It seemed that in his buck-fevered moment, he forgot to pull the trigger! This led to his new hunting nickname of *Click.*

God has given you everything you need to be successful today. You need only pull the trigger of faith.

DENNIS KIROUAC

Each agate is a story of discovery. Some are very similar as well as somewhat unpolished. Some of them were taken from deep water, yet each is special and unique. Here are some agates that I found over the years.

Back in the 1970s, I sailed Lake Huron with my wife's uncle Walter Kidd (yes, we had "Captain Kidd"), his son-in-law Gary Slater, and a former coast guard captain whose name I can't recall, on Walt's newly acquired 28' Catalina sail boat. This required us to sail from Saginaw Bay, Michigan to Mackinaw City before Memorial Day (a spring sail).

Day one, we would sail from Saginaw to Oscoda. Day two, we make a run from Oscoda to Rogers City which would get us in around midnight. Day three, Rogers City to Mackinaw City. Right from the start, we all knew this would be difficult. We were sailing in six to eight-foot seas away from the site of shore in shipping lanes. All we could rely on was our maps, compass headings, and our watches in order to calculate our positions.

The lake was really wild for the first couple of days. On the second day, I had the night shift. What an experience—high winds, high seas, and all was dark except three lights. One light showed the tattler strings, which confirmed the wind direction in relation to the sail; the second came from the compass, letting know my heading direction; the third came from a little sensor indicating our hull speed. We would hold a certain heading at certain speed for a certain amount of time and plot on our map our approximate location. We had to add to this calculation one more important factor—"drift." Lake Huron is basically a huge river which runs down to Lake Erie, so all the while we were holding our compass heading, the lake below was moving us off our course. We would sail for a certain amount of time at one heading then change our course and run a certain amount of time to compensate for this ever-constant condition.

All of life is like this; we start out on a certain course, only to "drift" off course. Peoples, societies, nations, even churches start off in one direction only to lose their way over time. This all happens in moments and is very slight alteration. One-degree drift per inch is only seventeen thousandth of an inch (your hair is about three thousandth of an inch. You do the math). Not much per inch, but how about a hundred miles? Over time and tides of life, we are all battered off course. Without even realizing it, we can find ourselves lost.

Thankfully today, we have GPS, and one now can know exactly where they are at any time. They can even enter in coordinates, and the boat will steer itself to port. That works great for boats but not so for people. People wish that they had a GPS for life as they attempt to navigate their futures. Well, there is a GPS (God's Positioning System) available and has been here since the beginning. God has offered guidance since the start. We only need to hear and obey (another word for obey is agree). God has given you a free will, which means you are the master and commander of your own ship. He offers you on-the-spot guidance to sail through the most treacherous of storms and reefs that are out there. He promises that He will never leave you or forsake you and that he will guide you to His safe harbor in His heart. The main map he offers is the Bible; the compass is His Holy Spirit. If you will lean not on your own understanding but acknowledge Him in all your ways, He will direct your path.

"Not many of you should become teachers, my fellow believers, because you know that we who teach will be judged more strictly" (James 3:1, NIV).

Matthew 3:8–10 address this very well.

> *Produce fruit in keeping with repentance. And do not think you can say to yourselves, 'We have Abraham as our father.' I tell you that out of these stones God can raise up children for Abraham. The ax is already at the root of the trees, and every tree that does not produce good fruit will be cut down and thrown into the fire.*

The fruit of repentance is not rooted in Abraham's seed. We cannot give away fruit that we ourselves are not rooted in. This connection between root and fruit is the basis of all teaching relationships. And all teaching relationships are for producing change.

The motto of Apple is "Think differently." Isn't it interesting that Apple's icon is the image of an apple with a bite out of it? Satan planted the seed of a new thought about an existing thought, and Eve saw that it's fruit looked good even though she didn't know it's true root condition (this became a new inward root that drove her outward fruit). Remember, what you know or are rooted in you can control but what you know and are rooted in also controls you. The devil's scheme is to separate you and I from God. His only way to do this is to get you to do the moving one thought at a time.

"Your thoughts have brought you to where you are today and your thoughts will take you to where you will be tomorrow" (Lane). The truth is that all of our thoughts have brought us to this very place where we now stand. I am reminded that I am to take and make every thought captive to the obedience of Christ. Why? Otherwise those thoughts *will* take me captive and take me places I really don't want to go and pay a price it didn't want to pay for a lot longer time than I thought I'd have to pay it.

Once we move, we are cut off from God's presence, and we are in sin, which is a state of separation.

> *"I am the true vine, and my Father is the gardener. He cuts off every branch in me that bears no fruit, while every branch that does bear fruit he prunes so that it will be even more fruitful"* (John 15:1–2, NIV).

For those of us who are rooted in Christ, we still will be cut but in a good way.

Thoreau said it best (and I paraphrase it): "While thousands thrash away at the leaves of evil only one lays an axe to the root."

All desirable as well as undesirable behaviors are a byproduct of a root/fruit situation. Thrashing away at the leaves only "prunes" the situation and only delays a mighty comeback. The humble man must be in a low attitude in order to see and direct the axe of truth to the root. Remember, "No root…no fruit."

Sin is not bad or good behavior but rather without God's influence or resource. Either we are in Christ or we are not.

> You are already clean because of the word I have spoken to you. Remain in me, as I also remain in you. No branch can bear fruit by itself; it must remain in the vine. Neither can you bear fruit unless you remain in me.
>
> I am the vine; you are the branches. If you remain in me and I in you, you will bear much

fruit; apart from me you can do nothing. If you do not remain in me, you are like a branch that is thrown away and withers; such branches are picked up, thrown into the fire and burned. If you remain in me and my words remain in you, ask whatever you wish, and it will be done for you. This is to my Father's glory, [That's the invisible made visible] that you bear much fruit, *showing yourselves to be my disciples.* (John 15:3–8, NIV)

Jesus is the vine who is rooted in the Father, and we are grafted through the adoption process or more appropriately we are born again. We are His branches, and what are branches for? They are for branching out and bearing fruit.

I believe that it is God's intention for all of mankind to be fruitful and multiply, not just in people but in the fruit of the Spirit. I think He wants you and I to subdue the earth with that fruit.

We all live from moment to moment and just like a river, we are ever-flowing forward and our thoughts are ever-changing as we pick up new understandings and influences along our course. These events reside in our memories and are categorized by establishing filters which then assign meaning both rational and emotional (irrational), allowing assumptions to become facts so we can conclude based on that experience and our own biased history as to how we should respond. In essence, we actually look at our present and future through our past.

Imagine that you wearing eyeglasses. The glasses represent the sum total of all your experiences to date. Your lenses are shaped by your past to give you the clarity you need in order to negotiate your present and future. Everyone you meet has this lens structure; therefore, no one really sees the same present or future the same way or completely. This is why we are often in conflict with one another. We are constantly trying to get everyone else see through our glasses because in our opinion, we are seeing it clearly. God knows that man's thoughts are not His thoughts and man's way (of thinking and acting) are not His way. That is why we must be guided into all truth by the only one that can guide us—the Holy Spirit and God's Holy Word.

Another way of saying this is by the Bible parable about the man building his house on the rock versus the sand. Each new experience serves as either polishing our lens or reshaping them lens slightly or dramatically. This amends or updates it via the reflective loop and either way the memory is always altered and after many generations of similar experiences the original is lost. The house of understanding that we build can either be built on the continuing shifting sand of memories or on the bedrock of unmovable (truth).The first cannot stand the storms that demand for clear and factual recall. Only that which is built on a bed rock of unmovable (truth) will stand. The Bible is the only unshakable rock.

"When I was a Child, I spoke as a child, I understood as a child, I thought as a child; but when I became a man, I put away childish things" (1 Corinthians 13:11).

When you are born, two basic learning paths begin immediately. The first is the emotional-reactionary; the second is the reasoning-deliberating. The emotional has to do with survival—first contact—fight, flight, or freeze. The second has to do with the experiential-evaluate-learn.

An example would be learning to ride a bicycle. Initially your emotional kicks in as you face the challenge of your first attempt to ride. Because you have personally never had any prior experience, your tendency is to awfullize your potential outcomes of this upcoming event, even though successful examples abound encouraging you to push off. Once you initiate the experience, which most often accompanies large overemotional nonverbal as well as motor over-compensations, the experience begins to overwrite all prior assumptions. A week later, "Look, Mom, no hands!"

Experts say that until you are in your late twenties, the balance between the emotional and reasoning side have not hit an equilibrium, so until then the tendency is to feel things before you think things. Of course this can vary depending upon the amounts of new experiences one has received.

To say it another way is to imagine a kite. The main sail part is your emotional filter. The tail is your experiences. The string is your will. As life comes at you, one has to learn how to negotiate this ever-changing weather in order to maintain the right altitude (attitude). You require all three to be working together in order to soar over your challenges. If you had no tail, your sail portion would go in circles or rather a cycle of up than down. If you had only a tail, then you would never rise up over your situation no matter how much will power you exert. As you can see, this is not a situation you can fix but rather a tension to be managed. Learning when to pull back or to let go is an essential requirement in maturing the fruit of self control. Please know that the string is meant to be attached to the cross framework which both the sail and tail are to attached. You are to submit your will too and through the cross.

Humpty Dumpty sat on a wall. Humpty Dumpty had a great fall. All the king's horses and all the king's men couldn't put Humpty together again.

There is a huge truth to this children's rhyme. All of history is full of man's attempt to lay foundations of thinking other than what was originally laid. Upon these foundations, we have built walls of understanding which in turn creates compartmentalized rooms of belief. Any belief other than that is cast out as untrue or dangerous. These rooms are evident everywhere man is—countries, nations, regions, states, cities, towns, homes, schools. On and on, it plays out even to gender race, creed, and color. This fractured fairytale is the very nature of sin. Sin is a divider of the heart, mind, and soul. It pits all of man internally against himself as well as others. Each feels that his or her thoughts are right, and all others don't understand and need to be enlightened, corrected, or fixed in some way. God's way is not man's way nor is God's thoughts man's thought. There is a way that seems right to a man, but in the end it leads to death. Our only hope is found in the last phrase of the rhyme, "All the king's horses and all the king's men couldn't put Humpty together again." This is a job that only the King can do.

Lean not unto you own understanding, but in all your ways, acknowledge Him, and He will direct your path. That way, you will build right on the right foundation which has been laid from the beginning—a wall whose cornerstone is Christ Jesus.

The only thing that qualifies one for leadership is understanding. One cannot lead what one does not understand. Solomon asked for wisdom (understanding), and because of that, all else was added because he was then equipped to lead all else that would follow.

As I pondered that thought, I am reminded of a time I was driving to church one afternoon. My eyes were drawn to the sidewalk to my right. I beheld a mother walking with her son. He appeared to be approximately fourteen years of age. His shaky and unsteady walk indicated some sort of special needs. She had both her arms wrapped around his left arm. Her head was tilted carefully beside his left ear. It was obvious that she was both encouraging and giving direction. The young man clutched tightly with both hands to the white cane. I could see that he was struggling to negotiate the sidewalk. At once, God said to me. This mother represents the Holy Spirit and His relationship to me and every person. I believe that the mother has all kinds of hopes and dreams for her little traveler. She could see and understand clearly what is about to come and knows what must be done in order to negotiate with the ever changing landscape. She knew that her son could only see and understand through the narrow bandwidth of his cane. She also knows that true direction can only be brought through a close and gentle whisper. God said He sees what I cannot and that I need to trust the gentle touch of His Spirit and heed the soft whisper of His voice and that through the narrow bandwidth of faith, I need to hear, trust and obey. He said, "Lean not unto your own understanding, but in all my ways acknowledge Me and I will direct your path."

We are all blind, and we are all without understanding. The only way we can navigate this life is in the ability to hear God and trust and obey (another word for obey would be agree). Having the power to hear God's voice allows us to negotiate everything we encounter. We live in an ever-changing situation which never is the exact same; therefore, we can never really be fully understanding and prepared.

The Holy Spirit is called the Spirit of Truth. When Adam and Eve ate of the fruit, they ate from the tree of the knowledge of good and evil. They received only conceptual knowledge. Knowledge is not truth. God's Word says, "Taste and see that the Lord is good." Seeing is supposed to mean understanding, but you and I know that we often see but do not understand. However, when we taste something, we understand immediately. Many of us see only, have knowledge, but not the experience which gives us understanding.

Even though I am blind, it does not mean that I am not without resource to see.

The main requirement for leadership is understanding.

"You cannot lead what you don't understand."
"You cannot understand what you have not experienced."
"You cannot experience what you haven't tried."
"You cannot try what unless you had a vision."
"You cannot have a vision without a dream."
"You cannot have a dream without a hope for the future."
"You cannot have a hope for the future without a hunger."
In today's society, we have great abundance.
No hunger, therefore no hope, and the order is reversed.

Olive oil in Jesus's day was probably more valuable that black oil is today. Oil was used to anoint kings and for healing. Oil was used for food and for light. The process to make this oil was very simple.

Step 1: Gather olives from the trees.
Step 2: Place into the olive press station where a large basin and a large stone wheel usually drawn by a donkey to break open the olives.
Step 3: Gather the mush produced in the previous step and place them into specially made baskets.
Step 4: Place twelve of these baskets on top of each other.

Most pure of the three steps and would only be used for anointing and healing. Step 2 is where the baskets were move to another vat station #2 where a flat stone would be placed on top of the baskets and weight would be added. This would produce a lesser grade oil for food and cooking. The third and final step is again to move the baskets to a third vat station, add even more weight, and produce oil usually used for lamp light fuel.

This process is very symbolic in nature:

Step 1: God gathers us from the world.
Step 2: God breaks us (our hearts).
Step 3: God regathers in churches.
Step 4: God crushes us and out of this crushing comes our anointing to be able and enabled to

1. *Reach up* through worship and prayer which is the first fruits or oil of anointing.
2. *Reach out* to help gather lost in this dying world.
3. *Reach around* through service and sacrifice to feed and show God's light to these new children so they too can find their anointing.

In Genesis, we read the story of God creating the heavens, earth, and of course man. At the end of each day, He would proclaim, "It is good." However, when it came to man, He proclaimed, "It is not good that man should be alone." So God put the man in a deep sleep and removed his rib, and from this rib, he formed the woman. Basically what God did was to incomplete the man, and out of this incompleteness, He forms the woman. Today, everyone is talking about sameness; women want to be the same as men, men want to be the same as women. This is no new thing; in fact that is exactly what Satan offered man in the garden of Eden. "If you eat of this fruit, you will be just like God in the knowledge of good and evil." Who wouldn't want to be just like God?

Here's a thought: go before a mirror and put out your right arm. Notice that the image of that arm being reflected back is on the left hand side of the reflected body. In order for the reflection to have the arm on the "same" side, you would have to turn your back to the mirror. We are made in the God's image, not a sameness image but a reflective image. We were made to be a complementary, not same. So the only way to be exactly like God is to turn our back on Him. God said that the two shall become one. Man and woman were made to be in a complementary, not the sameness, relationship. They are completer's of each other, not the competitors of each other.

Another reason for this arrangement was that man was made in God's image and God is a creator of life and man couldn't create life. He could create names but not life. So God had to first break the man in order for man to be able to create life, thus the two become the one. Children represent the indivisible oneness of love between a man and woman, as well as the two being born again. That's why God hates divorce because it removes the complementary and produces sameness where completer's become competitors. This filters down to all of life and because of sin, which is basically the turning our backs to God, and is evidenced in everything we see.

"So what did we eat?"
"Fruit."
"What fruit?"
"The fruit of the knowledge of good and evil."

Fruit represents the end of a process. It looks nothing like the tree or it branches. Fruit is made to be attractive, free for the taking. It provides perceived sustenance or benefit to another. But within this fruit lies the seed of the continence of its root. Adam and Eve ate of a fruit with no knowledge of or experience of its root.

The tree of knowledge of good and evil was a tree that offered two choices that a being of free will must have in order to have a choice. One root/fruit was the good root whose fruit offers agape (unconditional love). The other root/fruit offers a performance-based Eros, philia, storge love. Evil is a mindset that is rooted through external validation striving to be fruited through achievement to become acceptable by their one's own efforts.

One offers complimentary, not sameness, while the other offers competitor, not completer.

That is how *evil* came into this world. Now evil is not images of bad behaviors, but rather evil is a mindset or way of thinking. Proverbs 23:7 states, "For as he thinketh in his heart, so is he."

Evil is short for this: Ego-Validation-Identity-Love.

So by turning our backs on God, who is light, we gaze into to unknown darkness, and out of fear of the unknown our *ego* looks for *validation* from other sources than God in order to create an *identity* in order to be accepted or *loved*. From piercings to tattoos to a three-piece suit and a Ghurka briefcase, our behaviors are driven by this set of evil values. A good example would be an athlete who spends time, treasure, and talent in order to *validate* and achieve an *identity* as a world-class athlete, which in turns gives them respect admiration and *love* from other sources than the originator—God.

But God has called us to *repent* which means to turn around and go the other way. So let's reverse the order. By turning toward God, we find that *love* (agape unconditional love) is our *identity* that *validates* our *ego*. Just like our children, it doesn't matter what these little beezers or beezerettes do, they will never cease to be our children.

The same is for you and me. It doesn't matter what you and I have done, God is still our Father, and we can't change that truth anymore than our children can change their DNA.

What is so important to know is that we are not human beings having a spiritual experience but rather spiritual beings having a human experience. On the natural, God has created life on this plane to reveal His glory which means the invisible made visible. He has created man to walk along side Him so he can guide and teach him of all of His truths. His plan, because man is not eternal, only his spirit, is to go from generation to generation, teaching each generation to pass on what they have learned to the next, and God will add to each new generation new insights to His truths. Since God is without end, so is this process. We are to go from glory to glory.

God is king. His kingdom reigns forever.

God has a kingdom, not a republic, not a democracy—a kingdom. Kingdom is short for a king's domain. The king and queen representing a complimentary relationship together were responsible, meaning they had the ability to respond to use their resource of power to provide and protect all within the realm. From highest to the least, no one would be forgotten.

When one came before the king, they were at the king's digression, either to be set to his right hand, signifying they are under his power, provision, and protection or to his left, signifying they were not of his kingdom responsibility. In many cultures, both ancient and modern, the right hand is considered clean, and the left hand is unclean.

The Bible says that Jesus is seated at the right hand of the Father and that we are seated with Christ in heavenly places. This means that all we have to offer Jesus is our left hand, our uncleanness. Jesus, who is clean, has taken on our uncleanness and has gone before the Father representing us. Because He sits at the Father's right hand, all power, provision, and protection is given to Him, and He in turn conveys all power, provision, and protection to us—which we in turn are supposed to do for others.

The marriage ceremony is the perfect symbolic picture of God's kingdom and His plan of salvation. The pastor would represent God the King, and the groom's family would be seated to his right, the bride's family to the left.

The bride is guided down the aisle to be presented to the pastor holding onto her father's right arm, signifying his power of provision and protection for her. He also would be standing between the groom's family while she remained on her family side. The groom was to stand to the left of the pastor, and the bride would be placed to the pastor's right. This positioning would set the stage of the transfer of responsibility through the pastor from her father to her husband for the power, provision, and protection for her. This also is a great picture of the bride of Christ which is the church. The two of them would create a new identity representing the rebirth of a new life (she would get a new name or identity). Together, the groom would walk out from the pastor's presence with the wife holding onto his right arm, signifying that he is now responsible for power of provision and protection for her.

Life is like a dance. In order to dance, you need a partner. The first dance at the wedding reception is very descriptive of how man and wife relationship is to function. First, the man extends his left hand, palm up which is revealing the vulnerable underside of his weakness. She in turn is to place her right hand over his left, signifying that she is to use her power, provision, and protection to cover him in his weakness. Next she places her left hand on his right shoulder, which signifies that he is to use his whole right side of his body of power, provision, and protection to shoulder and support her in her weakness. Finally he is to place his right hand, palm out to cover his rib that she was made from which signifies his power, provision, and protection of her heart. Next she would step back with her right foot, signifying she will humble herself and allow him to lead with his left foot, representing his weakness which represents him allowing God to guide his steps. Together they shift to his right, her left, to set the next move to allow her to lead and he to follow. This all leads back to where their started, and just like their wedding rings, it creates a seamless unbroken dance which will carry them through a life of honoring and preferring.

The first miracle that Jesus did is of meaning. Imagine that you were about to launch a new business, and you are well aware that you never get a second chance to make a first impression. Your new initiative would need to differentiate itself from all competitors in such a way as to make choosing your way the best option. You need to be able to answer the questions of *why?*

Why a wedding?

He was beginning with the ending in mind. All of Jesus's miracles were for the expressed purpose of pointing us back to a new relationship and identity to God through a wedding process with would lead to creation of new life.

Why the interplay with Mary?

Every year Jesus' parents went to Jerusalem for the Festival of the Passover. When he was twelve years old, they went up to the festival, according to the custom. After the festival was over, while his parents were returning home, the boy Jesus stayed behind in Jerusalem, but they were unaware of it. Thinking he was in their company, they traveled on for a day. Then they began looking for him among their relatives and friends. When they did not find him, they went back to Jerusalem to look for him. After three days they found him in the temple courts, sitting among the teachers, listening to them and asking them questions. Everyone who heard him was amazed at his understanding and his answers. When his parents saw him, they were astonished.

His mother said to him, "Son, why have you treated us like this? Your father and I have been anxiously searching for you."

"Why were you searching for me?" he asked. "Didn't you know I had to be in my Father's house?" But they did not understand what he was saying to them.

Then he went down to Nazareth with them and was obedient to them. But his mother treasured all these things in her heart. And Jesus grew in wisdom and stature, and in favor with God and man.

From that moment on, the Bible is silent, and you hear nothing more about Him until Mary intervenes on the third day of the wedding. Her final instructions were to the servants was to "*do whatever he tells you.*"

Jesus establishes that he will do ministry through willing servants, and without their cooperation, his work will not happen.

Why six stone water jars? The number six in the Bible refers to the number of man. Water signifies life. So there you have the symbol of man who is full of life.

Jesus than transforms the water to wine. Wine signifies "new life" or being born again.

I always wondered why they told the portion about the bringing of the wine to the master of the ceremony and this exchange between him and the groom about the wine protocol. But the answer to this is to show you how the world gives you its best, and after you have drunk enough, this world will give you its worst. But in God's kingdom, you come to Him at your worst, and He takes you from glory to glory to your best.

Like the fine parallel lines of an agate, the Bible is full of parallels as well. Throughout the Bible is a theme of the younger ruling over the older. Some examples are:

- Able over Cain
- Jacob over Esau
- Isaac over Ishmael
- Joseph over his ten older brothers
- Jesus over Adam

Last but not least are you and I. We must be born again, and that is where our old nature must be ruled over by our new nature.

> *Jesus answered, "Very truly I tell you, no one can enter the kingdom of God unless they are born of water and the Spirit. Flesh gives birth to flesh, but the Spirit gives birth to spirit. You should not be surprised at my saying, 'You must be born again.'* (John 3:5–7, NIV)

Another parallel of the born-again process is found in the Old Testament through Joseph. Israel is introduced into Egypt (Egypt represents flesh). Over the course of time, Egypt becomes pregnant with this nation of Israel as it kept growing to the point that it *would overtake Egypt. Now along comes Moses whose name* means *"I drew him out of water"* and is born of slavery, and through a basket experience to similar Noah's ark experience, he is born again to become the deliverer (birthing term) of Israel. The ten labor pains pushes Egypt to give birth to this new nation as the water breaks at the Red (Reed) Sea, and a new nation is birthed unto a desert. In Egypt, they had all resource and no God source, but in the desert, they had no resource but only God source. It takes forty more years to clean up the Egypt from Israel. Then Israel is born again as the water breaks again at the river Jordan. Israel takes their first steps to establish a nation where God will dwell. They are tested by three cities to conquer in order to establish God's kingdom but fail, which sets the stage for our one true deliver, Jesus. He is born as every man is. For nine months, he is in water. The water breaks and he receives his first breath of air as well as a name. He goes through life to be born again when he is baptized, and as he breaks forth from the water, he takes in his first breath of the Holy Spirit who descends upon Him, and a voice from on high says, "This is my son whom I am well pleased." He, like Israel, is led by the Holy Spirit into the desert to be tempted.

> *Then Jesus was led by the Spirit into the wilderness to be tempted by the devil. After fasting forty days and forty nights, he was hungry. The tempter came to him and said, "If you are the Son of God, tell these stones to become bread."*
>
> *Jesus answered, "It is written: 'Man shall not live on bread alone, but on every word that comes from the mouth of God.'"* (Matthew 4:1–4, NIV)

Had Jesus done what was suggested, He would have been known as the "Bread Messiah."

> *Then the devil took him to the holy city and
> had him stand on the highest point of the temple.
> "If you are the Son of God," he said, "throw yourself
> down. For it is written:*
> *"'He will command his angels concerning you,
> and they will lift you up in their hands, so that you
> will not strike your foot against a stone.'"*
> *Jesus answered him, "It is also written: 'Do not
> put the Lord your God to the test.'" (vv.5–7)*

Had Jesus done what was suggested, He would have been
known as "The Messiah of the Spectacular."

> *Again, the devil took him to a very high moun-
> tain and showed him all the kingdoms of the world
> and their splendor. "All this I will give you," he said,
> "if you will bow down and worship me."*
> *Jesus said to him, "Away from me, Satan! For
> it is written: 'Worship the Lord your God, and serve
> him only.'"*
> *Then the devil left him, and angels came and
> attended him. (vv.8–11)*

Finally had Jesus complied with Satan's request He would had
been known as "The compromising Messiah."

Just like the three encounters Israel faced in the promise land
which led to comprise by man to try and negotiate an agreement to

fast track the process, Jesus overcomes by putting His Father first by responding, "It is written, it is written, it is written." Then the Bible says the he left the desert under the power of the Holy Spirit. We now find Him doing miracles where He is feeding five thousand, being the bread messiah, raising the dead, the messiah of the spectacular, but He never compromises, even when face with death—death on a cross.

The final parallel leads you and I back to Nicodemus in the book of John.

> *"How can someone be born when they are old?" Nicodemus asked. "Surely they cannot enter a second time into their mother's womb to be born!"*
> (John 3:4–7, NIV)

It's the same path that Israel as a nation and Jesus as Savior walked as being two witnesses, establishing it as being so. You and I must travel this "way, the truth, the life." When we accept this truth in our life, we are baptized by both water and fire and are led to be tested as Jesus was, and after testing without compromising, we go out into this world under the power of His Holy Spirit.

Many times when I walked the beach, there would be large trees which had be ripped out from the roots, and all the bark would be gone. Sometimes they had been cut and probably washed down a river and out to the lake. When I was young, I would help the loggers out in the woods who were getting pulpwood for the paper mill in town. All of these trees started out as seeds, and over time through nature and nurture, they grew to maturity.

Some years back, I acquired some riverfront property which needed some seventy-seven trees to be harvested. I had the responsibility to take care of the tops as well as the stumps. This turned out to be a two-year project where I would every day "chip away." First the tops were cut for firewood to be given away. Next the stumps, which I would remove by hand through digging and chopping by Axe. Some of these stumps were three feet in diameter. As I worked these stumps, I learned the various root structures of different tree types, and I learned a great deal how the trees root to survive and thrive.

One day as I was removing one of the largest stumps, God said this is what the process of true forgiveness looks like. He said, "Imagine this yard is your heart, and someone offends you. This offence is a seed that is planted in your heart. Over time this seed, if not tended too, will grow through you, nurturing it with the resources of your heart to a point where it will become visible and eventually stand between you and the offender. Even though you try to overlook the offence, it will grow beyond your ability to see past."

Then He reminded me of where he responded to Peter in Matthew 18:21–22 (NIV):

> *Then Peter came to Jesus and asked, "Lord, how many times shall I forgive my brother or sister who sins against me? Up to seven times?"*
>
> *Jesus answered, "I tell you, not seven times, but seventy-seven times.*

He then said that you only get offended once, but it is you remembering it 490 times that causes it to grow. To remove it through forgiveness by cutting down the tree of offence only removes what stands between you and the offender, but you still must negotiate going around its stump every time you mow.

It is still taking up room and resource in your heart. God said that I am to lay the axe of truth to every root in order to totally remove it. This is the true dying daily by refusing resource to the offence. God then said that offenses are much easier to deal with if you do it right away when it is in seed form. That way you don't have to keep a record of wrongs.

> *So, chosen by God for this new life of love, dress in the wardrobe God picked out for you: compassion, kindness, humility, quiet strength, discipline. Be even-tempered, content with second place, quick to forgive an offense. Forgive as quickly and completely as the Master forgave you. And regardless of what else you put on, wear love. It's your basic, all-purpose garment. Never be without it.*
> (Colossians 3:13–14, MSG)

It amazes me how God will use the everyday activities to speak truth of His kingdom.

Final Thought:

Hidden in the last book of the bible is this little known verse.

17 Whoever has ears, let them hear what the Spirit says to the churches.
To the one who is victorious, I will give some of the hidden manna.
I will also give that person a white stone with a new name written on it,
known only to the one who receives it.
(Revelation 2:17 NIV)

To all my fellow searchers, be encouraged with this tremendous promise.
All of searching is born of a true hunger.
The first of the three tests that Jesus had to face in the wilderness began with hunger. Satan did not lie when he said "Tell these stones to become bread". To all who are victorious you shall never hunger for your identity and your purpose will be fovever written on the white stone.

ABOUT THE AUTHOR

*F*inding *Agates* is Kirouac's accounts and insights into life on Lake Superior and how God reveals himself through everyday experiences in a delightful and thought-provoking ways.

CPSIA information can be obtained
at www.ICGtesting.com
Printed in the USA
JSHW030653090620
6117JS00004B/16